Copyright Local Government Association 2001

Published by LGA Publications, the Local Government Association,
Local Government House, Smith Square, London SW1P 3HZ.
Tel. 020 7664 3000. Fax. 020 7664 3030.

Price £20 (including postage) £10 to local authorities

Copies can be purchased from IDeA Publication Sales, Layden House,
76-86 Turnmill Street, London EC1M 5LG.
Tel. 020 7296 6600. Fax. 020 7296 6523.
Please quote LGA code SR027 and send cheque (made payable to 'IDeA')
with order.

LGA code SR027

ISBN 1 84049 228 7

Contents

Policy context and emerging themes

The government has confirmed its intention to give local authorities a new strengthened strategic housing role. In its housing policy statement of 13 December 2000 *The Way Forward for Housing*, the role of the Local Government Association (LGA) in leading the debate with its establishment of a task group on the future strategic housing role was acknowledged. The LGA's task group's report *Vision into Reality*, published in early December 2000[1], called on authorities to:

- embrace the strategic role as their primary housing function;

- ensure that housing becomes a central component of community strategies;

- develop their role as a 'champion' of housing consumers;

- reshape their relationships with registered social landlords;

- improve joint working between housing and planning;

- improve the strategic and operational links between housing, health and education.

This report details the results of a survey carried out by the LGA research team from November 2000 – February 2001 to find out how authorities are looking at the future strategic housing role and to explore some of the issues raised by the LGA's task group report. The survey is based on a 65 per cent response rate, providing a good cross-section of authorities across different regions.

The report includes an executive summary of the research findings, as well as some of the key themes to emerge.

Part 1 housing strategy

An overwhelming majority of authorities recognise the need to integrate housing strategies with the new duty to prepare community-wide strategies and, alongside integration with Local Strategic Partnerships, see this as a continuing priority over the next five years.

Supporting People - the new funding framework for providing housing support services to vulnerable people, to be introduced in April 2003 - was most commonly identified by authorities as the specific area which would be given higher priority in housing strategies over the next five years.

Nearly three-quarters of authorities anticipate that a key element of the housing consumer 'champion' role (facilitating or providing a wider range of services/support across housing tenures) will be an increasingly important priority in the future.

Education and health are also identified as areas of increasing priority in strategies by over one-third and around a half of authorities, respectively.

Practically all local authorities consulted Registered Social Landlords (RSLs) in preparing their housing strategies and around half of all local authorities stated that lettings policies of all social housing landlords and more involvement of RSLs in non-housing work would be more important in the next five years.

---

[1] Available from IDeA Publication Sales, tel 020 7296 6600, fax 020 7296 6523, price £20, £10 for member authorities, LGA code HO124. Also available on the LGA's website are discussion papers supporting the task group's findings and a joint LGA/CIH briefing note on modernising the legal basis for local authorities' strategic housing role. http://www.lga.gov.uk/lga/socialaffairs/housingindex.htm#Strategic

Local authority tenants were the most commonly cited user group consulted on formulating housing strategies. Black and minority ethnic communities (especially in rural areas) and private sector residents were the least consulted.

There is evidence of authorities becoming more sophisticated in their approach to housing market analysis. Well over half of authorities anticipate more joint working with planning departments and addressing issues on a cross-boundary bases. In the current year and over the next 12 months most authorities will have undertaken an analysis of the whole housing market across all sectors and over two thirds will have used new data sources.

Overall the survey shows that many authorities recognise both the breadth and increasing importance of the strategic housing role. There is still however, a need for this to be more widespread and for greater consultation with the wider community on the formulation of the housing strategy. For the many authorities who are taking a broad perspective the future challenge is to translate this into effective action and outcomes on the ground.

Part 2 housing services

Stock investment options

Forty five responding authorities envisage applying to go on the stock transfer programme over the next 18 months - this amounts to around 580,000 dwellings. A number of responding authorities are giving serious consideration to a range of investment options: 115 are giving serious consideration to Arms Length Housing Management Companies (ALHMC); 95 are

giving serious consideration to stock transfer and 60 authorities are giving serious consideration to the Private Finance Initiative (PFI). (These latter figures are not mutually exclusive - many authorities are considering more than one option). Forty three responding authorities are not considering alternative stock investment options at the moment.

Housing and neighbourhood management

Over a half of authorities who manage stock have 'on the spot' housing management in place and in half of these cases, these services are integrated with other neighbourhood services. Around one-quarter of authorities are planning to introduce neighbourhood management of local authority services (not just housing) in the next two years and in half of these authorities, the housing department is taking the lead role.

Best Value

Most authorities, particularly those in urban areas, have already carried out Best Value housing reviews, with housing management being the main service scrutinised. A smaller proportion of authorities have reviewed their strategic, enabling and homelessness roles. A majority of councils included working with RSLs within their Best Value Performance Plan, mainly through carrying out reviews of services or establishing benchmarking clubs.

Tenant participation

Three quarters of authorities had completed a tenant participation compact, the remainder being in progress or planned. (All authorities should have produced a tenant participation compact by April 2000). Most authorities consulted existing tenants on proposals for changing and improving services, monitoring arrangements and the housing strategy. Fewer councils consulted potential future tenants on these issues but some did. Customer satisfaction surveys were used by the majority of authorities.

Lettings

The majority of authorities have reviewed their allocation polices since the legislation governing lettings policies was last changed through the Housing Act 1996. However, in the light of the policy trend towards increasing customer choice in lettings, most councils are again reviewing, or plan to review, their policies. About a third of authorities already have common housing registers with RSLs and more are planned. Fewer authorities have, or plan to have, common allocations policies. Common registers are more likely to occur in rural than in urban areas. This is not surprising since the number of RSLs likely to be active in urban areas will generally be much greater.

Blanket exclusions from the housing register on a permanent basis were relatively small. Once the Homes Bill is enacted authorities will no longer be able to exclude whole groups of people from the register although they will be able to give a lower priority to certain types of cases and, subject to the right of review and under tightly defined circumstances, to exclude certain individuals from consideration for a tenancy on the grounds of unacceptable behaviour.

Most exclusions from the register were on the grounds of no local connection, closely followed by households who had been evicted for anti-social behaviour. Where households were excluded on the grounds of debt or rent owed the exclusion was either time limited or, in most cases, until the circumstances changed, presumably when the debt was either paid or when arrangements to pay had been agreed.

Advice services

The majority of authorities provided housing advice services directly, but nearly a fifth contracted out advice services, half of those councils who responded funded voluntary sector advice services and 10 per cent used the Community Legal Service. More than a third of authorities planned to expand their housing services in the light of the Housing Green Paper, which promotes a more active role for authorities in preventing homelessness through a broader approach to housing advice.

Summary of survey results

Housing strategy

Currently most authorities will have housing strategies with the following elements:

- joint work with Registered Social Landlords (99 per cent);

- energy efficiency (98 per cent);

- overall supply of housing (96 per cent);

- private sector housing renewal (94 per cent);

- private rented sector (94 per cent);

- community safety (92 per cent).

In the next five years authorities on the whole will see most of the elements of their housing strategies being more important or the same. Those elements that were seen as being of the highest priority in the next five years were:

- Supporting People (86 per cent);

- tenant participation and involvement (60 per cent);

- overall housing supply (58 per cent);

- neighbourhood renewal (57 per cent);

- social exclusion and anti-poverty (56 per cent).

Community strategies

- 82 per cent of authorities believe that the housing strategy will be well integrated in the community strategy which authorities will have a duty to prepare in the future;

- 91 per cent of housing departments are represented on the development of the community strategy.

Stakeholder involvement

The research asked authorities to indicate which stakeholders they consulted in preparing the housing strategy. The results show that authorities involve a wide range of stakeholders in preparing the strategy. Most authorities consulted:

- Registered Social Landlords (99 per cent);

- voluntary and community organisations (93 per cent);

- Housing Corporation (81 per cent);

- health authorities and trusts (81 per cent);

- Government Offices for the Regions (73 per cent).

Specific user groups

User consultation with different groups in formulating the strategy varied considerably. Those user groups who authorities tended to consult most were:

- local authority tenants (76 per cent);

- older people (43 per cent);

- people in or needing supported housing, people with disabilities, local authority leaseholders, Registered Social Landlord tenants (41 per cent).

Housing market analysis

An important element in developing the strategic housing role will be the ways in which authorities develop a range of techniques to understand local housing markets. Authorities are currently likely to see the following elements as most important:

- working with the planning department (93 per cent);

- addressing issues on a cross local authority boundary basis (56 per cent);

- involvement of a range of stakeholders (55 per cent);

- carrying out a housing needs survey (53 per cent);

- carrying out a stock condition survey (52 per cent).

Authorities are likely to see the following elements as most important in the next 12 months:

- working with the planning department (64 per cent);

- addressing issues on a cross local authority boundary basis (59 per cent);

- analysing the scope for the private sector to meet housing needs (55 per cent);

- involvement of a range of stakeholders (53 per cent).

Links with regional bodies

- 71 per cent of authorities have commented on the development of the regional housing statement. There are differences by regions of the country – Yorkshire & Humberside (100 per cent) to South East (61 per cent);

- 71 per cent of authorities have commented on the development of the Housing Corporation regional investment strategy. There are differences by regions of the country – Yorkshire & Humberside (91 per cent) to South West (57 per cent;

- 64 per cent of authorities are aware of a regional body to represent their views. There are differences by regions of the country - London (94 per cent) to East Midlands (27 per cent).

Priorities for the future

Authorities are most likely to see priorities for next five years as being:

- integrating housing with community strategies (92 per cent);

- integrating housing with Local Strategic Partnerships (84 per cent);

- facilitating or providing a wider range of services/support across housing tenures (71 per cent);

- building sustainable communities (65 per cent);

- ways to modernise and fund local authority stock renewal (60 per cent).

Partnerships

Partnership working will be a key component of the future strategic housing role. The majority of authorities believe that all partners will be more important or the same in importance to work with over the next five years. The partners local authorities see as being more important to work with over the next five years are:

- RDAs and regional assemblies (70 per cent);

- health sector (69 per cent);

- neighbouring local authorities (68 per cent).

Housing services

Stock investment options

- 27 per cent of authorities who responded to the survey have transferred dwellings to a RSL, housing company or other landlord;

- of the remaining respondents, 25 per cent of authorities are not considering alternative stock investment options at the moment; 25 per cent are considering Arms Length Housing Management Companies only; 25 per cent are considering Arms Length Housing Management Companies and PFI only; and 12 per cent are considering stock transfer only;

- 56% of authorities who responded to the survey are giving serious consideration to stock transfer in the next 18 months;

- 26 per cent of authorities who responded to the survey envisage going on the stock transfer programme in the next 18 months - this amounts to around 580,000 dwellings;

- 69 per cent (115) of authorities who responded to the survey are giving serious consideration to Arms Length Housing Management Companies and 56 per cent (95) to stock transfer (as indicated above a number of authorities are considering more than one option);

- 37 per cent (60) of authorities who responded to the survey are giving serious consideration to the Private Finance Initiative (PFI) (as indicated above a number of authorities are considering more than one option).

Housing and neighbourhood management

- 52 per cent of authorities who manage stock have 'on the spot' housing management in place at the **estate level**;

- 59 per cent of authorities who manage stock have 'on the spot' housing management in place at the **neighbourhood level**;

- 51 per cent of these neighbourhood management services are integrated with other local authority or agency services;

- 21 per cent of authorities already have a neighbourhood warden scheme in place, and a further 34 per cent plan to introduce this in the next two years;

- 18 per cent of authorities have some form of estate agreements with Registered Social Landlords on joint management in rented housing, and a further 19 per cent plan this in the future;

- six per cent of authorities have plans for neighbourhood management of local authority services, and a further 24 per cent plan to introduce this in the next two years;

- of those authorities developing neighbourhood management, 48 per cent are being led through the housing department, and 52 per cent through a corporate unit.

Best Value

- 75 per cent of authorities have already undertaken reviews this year on housing services ;

- 40 per cent of planned Best Value reviews are on housing management; 12 per cent on the strategic/enabling role; 10 per cent on homelessness; seven per cent on private sector work; and six per cent on housing advice;

- 77 per cent of authorities have produced a tenant participation compact, with a further 18 per cent having this in progress;

- 92 per cent of authorities have involved councils tenants through customer satisfaction surveys; 92 per cent through proposals for changing and improving services; 85 per cent through being involved in decisions on the housing strategy; and 81 per cent on monitoring performance;

- 48 per cent of authorities have involved potential tenants in customer satisfaction surveys; 43 per cent on proposals for changing and improving services; 21 per cent on decisions on the housing strategy; and 16 per cent on monitoring performance;

- 67 per cent of authorities have included working with Registered Social Landlords in their Best Value Performance Plan;

- 79 per cent of authorities worked with RSLs on carrying out reviews of services; 70 per cent on benchmarking clubs; and 32 per cent on new approaches to tenant participation.

Choice in lettings/nominations policies

- 87 per cent of authorities have undertaken a review of allocation policies since the 1996 Housing Act;

- 41 per cent are currently reviewing allocation policies in light of the Housing Green Paper, and a further 36 per cent plan to review this in the next 12 months;

- 34 per cent of authorities have a Common Housing Register with RSLs, and a further 14 per cent have this planned in the next 12 months;

- 13 per cent have a Common Allocations Policy with RSLs, and a further 11 per cent have this planned for the next 12 months;

- 38 per cent have plans for local lettings policies, with a further 33 per cent planning to look at local lettings policies. Of those who responded 'yes', 50 per cent said they only applied to council housing, and the other 50 per cent to cross-sector housing;

- on the whole local authorities are flexible about exclusions from the housing register. 16 per cent are excluded on a permanent basis through a lack of residential qualification; 12 per cent evicted for anti-social behaviour; five per cent for a criminal conviction; and three per cent for rent arrears or other debts owed;

- of those who are a stock transfer authority, 49 per cent have the housing register in-house, and 51 per cent contract it out.

Housing advice services

- 87 per cent of authorities said housing advice services were provided directly by the local authority; 49 per cent said they gave funding to advice services; 17 per cent said it was contracted out; and 10 per cent used the Community Legal Service;

- 38 per cent of authorities are planning to expand housing advice services in light of the Housing Green Paper.

Survey results
Part 1: housing strategy

Elements of the housing strategy

The research wanted to establish what elements authorities used in their existing housing strategies. We asked authorities to indicate which elements were in the housing strategy and the results are shown in Table 1.

Currently most authorities will have housing strategies with the following elements:

- joint work with Registered Social Landlords (99 per cent);
- energy efficiency (98 per cent);
- overall supply of housing (96 per cent);
- private sector housing renewal (94 per cent);
- private rented sector (94 per cent);
- community safety (92 per cent).

Table 1: Current elements of the housing strategy

Element	% who have this in strategy	Urban/rural figures %
Joint working with Registered Social Landlords	99	99/98
Energy efficiency	98	98/99
Overall supply of housing in relation to requirements	96	97/91
Private sector housing renewal	94	95/93
Private rented sector	94	95/93
Community safety	92	94/89
Housing and health improvement	88	88/87
Advice services	87	88/87
Single homelessness/rough sleeping	87	89/85
Social exclusion/anti-poverty	85	88/82
Supporting People	85	87/81
Tenant participation/involvement	82	89/72
Affordable rents	77	75/78
Needs of owner-occupiers	74	76/70
Improving management of local authority housing	74	83/60
Strategy for ant-social behaviour	73	81/62
Equal opportunities	71	74/66
Housing linked to employment/training	69	77/57
Renewal of local authority housing stock	69	82/49
Neighbourhood renewal	61	75/41
Housing and education/children/youth	59	62/54
Asylum seekers/refugees	54	65/36
Registered Social Landlords' performance	54	56/51

Base: 223

The research was also interested to discover about the priorities for the next five years, and the responses are shown in Table 2.

In the next five years authorities on the whole will see most of the elements of their housing strategies being more important or the same. Those elements that were seen as being of the **highest priority** in the next five years were:

- Supporting People (86 per cent);

- tenant participation and involvement (60 per cent);

- overall housing supply (58 per cent);

- neighbourhood renewal (57 per cent);

- social exclusion and anti-poverty (56 per cent).

Table 2: Priority for elements of strategy in next 5 years

Element	Higher	Same	Less	Urban/Rural differences – Higher priorty
Supporting People	86	10	4	91/79
Tenant participation/involvement	60	37	3	60/59
Overall supply of housing in relation to requirements	58	42	0	62/52
Neighbourhood renewal	57	38	5	62/45
Social exclusion/anti-poverty	56	41	3	61/49
Strategy for anti-social behaviour	54	41	5	56/52
Improvement management of local authority housing	52	44	4	56/43
Community safety	50	49	1	52/46
Registered Social Landlords' Performance	50	47	3	51/47
Renewal of local authority housing stock	49	49	2	49/49
Housing and health improvement	47	49	2	52/39
Housing linked to employment/training	42	51	7	43/41
Affordable rents	42	54	4	45/37
Joint working with Registered Social Landlords	41	56	3	38/46
Private rented sector	40	57	3	40/39
Private sector housing renewal	37	61	2	40/32
Single homelessness/rough sleeping	36	60	4	37/35
Housing and education	35	59	6	42/25
Advice services	31	65	4	29/35
Equal opportunities	31	66	3	36/24
Energy efficiency	30	68	2	34/23
Needs of owner-occupiers	30	65	5	35/22
Asylum seekers/refugees	29	51	20	34/19

Base: 223

Links with community strategies

- 82 per cent of authorities agree that the housing strategy will be well integrated in the community strategy which authorities will have a duty to prepare in the future (Table 3);

- 91 per cent of housing departments are represented on the development of the community strategy (Table 4).

Table 3: Degree to which housing strategy will be well integrated into the community strategy

	%
Strongly agree	35
Agree	47
Neither agree nor disagree	15
Disagree	2
Strongly disagree	1

Base: 222

Table 4: Is housing represented on the development of the community strategy within your authority?

	%
Yes	91
No	9

Base: 222

Stakeholder involvement

The research asked authorities to indicate which stakeholders they consulted in preparing the housing strategy. The results show that authorities involve a wide range of stakeholders in preparing the strategy (Table 5). Most authorities consulted:

- Registered Social Landlords (99 per cent);
- voluntary and community organisations (93 per cent);
- Housing Corporation (81 per cent);
- health authorities and trusts (81 per cent);
- Government Offices for the Regions (73 per cent).

Table 5: Stakeholders who were consulted in preparing housing strategy

Stakeholder	%	Urban/Rural Differences
Registered Social Landlords	99	100/99
Voluntary and community organisations	93	93/92
Housing Corporation	81	76/88
Health authorities and trusts	81	82/79
Government Offices for the Regions	73	69/79
Private landlords	65	63/69
Private developers/landowners	63	65/60
Police	61	61/63
Advice centres	60	58/62
Primary care groups	58	57/59
Neighbouring local authorities	50	41/61
Probation service	49	48/50
Building societies, banks, estate agents	43	39/49
Regional Development Agencies	15	14/17

Base: 221

Other stakeholders who were mentioned by responding authorities included local residents; parish councils; social services; and educational institutions and schools.

Specific user groups

The research asked which user groups had been consulted in formulating the housing strategy and these are shown in Table 6. User consultation with different groups in formulating the strategy varied considerably. Those user groups who authorities tended to consult most were:

- local authority tenants (76 per cent);

- older people (43 per cent);

- people in or needing supported housing, people with disabilities, local authority leaseholders, Registered Social Landlord tenants (each 41 per cent).

Table 6: User groups who have been consulted in formulating housing strategy

User group	%	Urban/Rural Differences %
Local authority tenants	76	85/62
Older people	43	46/40
People in or needing supported housing	41	45/36
People with disabilities	41	43/34
Local authority leaseholders	41	49/30
Registered Social Landlords tenants	41	39/42
Young people	37	36/39
Private tenants	33	38/23
Black and minority ethnic communities	29	40/13
Owner occupiers	28	34/21
Registered Social Landlord leaseholders	14	16/10
Private leasholders	12	13/9
Private tenants	12	

Base: 216

Other user groups who were mentioned by responding authorities included housing waiting list applicants; private landlords; and local residents groups.

Housing market analysis

An important element in developing the strategic housing role will be the ways in which authorities develop a range of techniques to understand local housing markets and these are shown in Table 7. Authorities are currently likely to see the following elements as most important:

- working with the planning department (93 per cent);

- addressing issues on a cross LA boundary basis (56 per cent);

- involvement of a range of stakeholders (55 per cent);

- carrying out a housing needs survey (53 per cent);

- carrying out a stock condition survey (52 per cent).

Table 7: Current elements of housing market analysis – carried out in the last 12 months

Element	%	Urban/Rural Differences %
Working with the planning department	93	93/91
Addressing issues on a cross LA boundary basis	56	60/50
Involvement of a range of stakeholders	55	57/51
Carrying out a housing needs survey	53	52/54
Carrying out a stock condition survey	52	53/49
Analysing the scope for the private sector to meet housing needs	47	47/47
Undertaking analysis of the whole local housing market across all sectors	44	45/42
Analysis of sub-regional and regional context	41	40/42
Using new data sources	31	33/29
Analysing interactions between different sectors	29	36/19
Analysing the scope for improving efficiency and effectiveness of private sector in meeting these needs	26	24/29
Adopting new techniques for analysis	23	29/16

Base: 231

The research also asked about the future elements of housing market analysis which authorities may use in the next 12 months and these are shown in Table 8. Authorities are likely to see the following elements as most important in the next 12 months:

- working with the planning department (64 per cent);

- addressing issues on a cross LA boundary basis (59 per cent);

- analysing the scope for the private sector to meet housing needs (55 per cent);

- involvement of a range of stakeholders (53 per cent)

Table 8: Future elements of housing market analysis in the next 12 months

Element	%	Urban/Rural Differences %
Working with the planning department	64	66/61
Addressing issues on a cross LA boundary basis	59	60/57
Analysing the scope for the private sector to meet housing needs	55	58/51
Involvement of a range of stakeholders	53	54/53
Carrying out a stock condition survey	49	51/46
Undertaking analysis of the whole local housing market across all sectors	47	49/44
Adopting new techniques for analysis	47	47/48
Carrying out a housing needs survey	42	40/44
Analysing the scope for improving efficiency and effectiveness of private sector in meeting these needs	41	41/40
Using new data sources	41	46/33
Analysing interactions between different sectors	39	39/37
Analysis of sub-regional and regional context	35	38/34

Base: 230

Links with regional bodies

- 71 per cent of authorities have commented on the development of the regional housing statement. There are differences by regions of the country – Yorkshire & Humberside (100 per cent) to West Midlands (44 per cent) (Table 9);

- 71 per cent of authorities have commented on the development of the Housing Corporation regional investment strategy. There are differences by regions of the country – Yorkshire & Humberside (91 per cent) to South West (57 per cent (Table 10);

- 64 per cent of authorities are aware of a regional body to represent their views. There are differences by regions of the country – London (94 per cent) to East Midlands (27 per cent) (Table 11).

Table 9: Have you commented on development of regional housing statement?

Region	% responded Yes
Yorkshire & Humberside	100
North West	93
East Midlands	79
North East	78
Eastern	72
London	69
South West	67
South East	61
West Midlands	44
ALL REGIONS	**71**

Base: 223

Table 10: Have you commented on development of the Housing Corporation regional investment strategy?

Region	% responded Yes
Yorkshire & Humberside	91
London	87
North East	78
South East	76
West Midlands	75
Eastern	73
North West	70
East Midlands	62
South West	57
ALL REGIONS	**71**

Base: 223

Table 11: Are you aware of any regional body representing the views of local government in your area to the Government Office for the region and Housing Corporation offices?

Region	% responded Yes
London	94
North East	87
North West	86
West Midlands	75
Yorkshire & Humberside	73
Eastern	65
South East	62
South West	46
East Midlands	27
ALL REGIONS	**64**

Base: 232

Priorities for the future

An important part of this research has been to seek the views from authorities on the priorities for the strategic housing role and the results are shown in Table 12.

Authorities are most likely to see priorities for the next five years as being:

- integrating housing with community strategies (92 per cent);

- integrating housing with local strategic partnerships (84 per cent);

- facilitating or providing a wider range of services/support across housing tenures (71 per cent);

- building sustainable communities (65 per cent);

- ways to modernise and fund local authority stock renewal (60 per cent).

Table 12: Priorities for future strategic housing role in next five years

Element	More important	Same	Less important	Urban/Rural differences % More important
Integrating housing with community strategies	92	8	0	92/93
Integrating housing with Local Strategic Partnerships	84	16	0	84/84
Facilitating or providing a wider range of services/support across housing tenures	71	27	2	71/71
Building sustainable communities	65	35	0	69/59
Ways to modernise and fund local authority stock renewal	60	29	11	69/47
Lettings policies of all social housing landlords	59	39	2	63/53
Working with regional bodies	58	41	1	61/43
Best Value	57	43	0	56/57
Managing supply and demand	56	43	1	62/48
Aligning housing with neighbourhood renewal strategies	50	46	4	59/36
More involvement of Registered Social Landlords in non-housing work	48	44	8	48/46
Private sector housing renewal	40	57	3	45/32
More emphasis on working with Registered Social Landlords	7	62	1	33/42

Base: 231

(Other areas mentioned as priorities for the next five years included the Housing Inspectorate; police; private landlords; and Primary Care Groups.)

Partnership working will be a key component of the future strategic housing role. The majority of authorities believe that all partners will be more important or the same in importance to work with over the next five years. Table 13 shows the partners local authorities see as being **more important** to work with over the next five years.

- RDAs and regional assemblies (70 per cent);
- health sector (69 per cent);
- neighbouring local authorities (68 per cent).

Table 13: Importance of different partners in the next 5 years in developing the strategic housing role

Element	More important	Same	Less important	Urban/Rural Differences % More important
RDAs and regional assemblies	70	30	0	74/64
Health sector	69	31	0	67/71
Neighbouring local authorities	68	31	1	67/68
Registered Social Landlords	50	50	0	50/50
Voluntary and community sector	49	51	0	50/49
Business sector	45	53	2	44/44
Housing Corporation	27	67	6	32/21
Learning and Skills Councils	27	70	3	28/25
Central government	27	68	5	26/28

Base: 231

Survey results
Part 2: housing services

Stock transfer investment options

- 27 per cent of authorities who responded to the survey have transferred dwellings to a RSL, housing company or other landlord (Table 15). Rural authorities are more likely to have transferred (40 per cent) than urban authorities (18 per cent). Stock transfers range from 53 per cent in the South East to 0 per cent in the North East;

- of the remaining respondents, 25 per cent of authorities are not considering alternative stock investment options at the moment; 25 per cent are considering Arms Length Housing Management Companies only; 25 per cent are considering Arms Length Housing Management Companies and PFI only; and 12 per cent are considering stock transfer only (Table 14);

- 56 per cent of authorities who responded to the survey are giving serious consideration to stock transfer in the next 18 months (Table 16);

- 26 per cent (45) of authorities who responded to survey envisage going on the stock transfer programme in the next 18 months - this amounts to around 580,000 dwellings (Table 17);

- 69 per cent (115) of authorities who responded to the survey are giving serious consideration to Arms Length Housing Management Companies (Table 18a) and 56 per cent (95) to stock transfer (Table 16) (as indicated above a number of authorities are considering more than one option);

- 37 per cent (60) of authorities who responded to the survey are giving serious consideration to the Private Finance Initiative (PFI) (Table 19) (as indicated above a number of authorities are considering more than one option).

Table 14: Stock transfer options

Option	%
Not considering any of the options	25
Arms Length Housing Management Company only	25
Arms Length Housing Management Company and PFI	25
Stock transfer only	12
Stock transfer and Arms Length Housing Management Only	6
Stock transfer, Arms Length Housing Management Company and PFI	3
PFI only	3
Stock transfer and PFI	*

Base: 171

Table 15: Authorities who have transferred dwellings to RSL/housing company/other landlord

Region	%
South East	53
South West	45
West Midlands	44
North West	20
Eastern	20
London	12
Yorkshire & Humberside	9
East Midlands	4
North East	0
ALL REGIONS	**27**

Base: 230 – 61 authorities said they had transferred stock

Table 16: Are you giving serious consideration to stock transfer in the next 18 months?

	%
Yorkshire & Humberside	90
North West	65
North East	62
West Midlands	58
Eastern	54
London	54
South West	50
East Midlands	43
South East	42
TOTAL ALL REGIONS	**56**

Base: 171 – 95 said they were considering stock transfer in the next 18 months

Table 17: Do you envisage going on the stock transfer programme in the next 18 months?

	%
Yes	26
No	74

Base: 156 – 45 said they envisage going on the programme

Table 18a Are you likely to give serious consideration to arms length local housing management companies)?

Region	%	
London	93	
Yorkshire & Humberside	80	
South East	78	
Eastern	73	
North West	67	
East Midlands	67	
South West	67	
West Midlands	54	
North East	44	
TOTAL ALL REGIONS	**69**	

Base: 163 – 115 authorities are considering ALHM

Table 18b Are you likely to give serious consideration to PFI in the future?

Region	%	
Yorkshire & Humberside	70	
London	62	
North West	46	
Eastern	38	
South East	31	
West Midlands	30	
North East	29	
South West	20	
East Midlands	19	
TOTAL ALL REGIONS	**37**	

Base: 156 – 60 authorities said they were considering PFI

Housing and neighbourhood management

- 52 per cent of authorities who manage stock have 'on the spot' housing management in place at the **estate level** (Table 19);

- 59 per cent of authorities who manage stock have 'on the spot' housing management in place at the **neighbourhood level** (Table 19);

- 51 per cent of these neighbourhood management services are integrated with other local authority or agency services (Table 20);

- 21 per cent of authorities already have a neighbourhood warden scheme in place, and further 34 per cent plan to introduce this in the next 2 years (Table 21);

- 18 per cent of authorities have some form of estate agreements with Registered Social Landlords on joint management in rented housing, and a further 19 per cent plan this in the future (Table 22);

- seven per cent of authorities have plans for neighbourhood management of local authority services, and a further 24 per cent plan to introduce this in the next two years (Table 23);

- of those authorities developing neighbourhood management, 48 per cent are being led through the housing department, and 52 per cent through a corporate unit (Table 24).

Table 19: Where your authority directly manages stock, do you already have or plan in the future, to have 'on the spot' housing management?

Estate level:

	%	Urban/Rural Differences %
Yes, already in place	52	62/29
No, but planned in the next 2 years	6	7/6
No, and not currently planned	42	31/65

Base: 163 (excludes authorities who do not manage stock)

Neighbourhood level

	%	Urban/Rural Differences %
Yes, already in place	59	65/48
No, but planned in the next 2 years	8	6/6
No, and not currently planned	34	29/46

Base: 163 (excludes authorities who do not manage stock)

Table 20: Are these services, currently or in the future, co-located or integrated with other local authority or agency services?

	%	Urban/rural differences %
Yes	51	54/40
No	49	46/60

Base: 160

Table 21: Do you already or plan in the future to have a neighbourhood warden scheme?

	%	Urban/rural differences %
Yes, already in place	21	27/12
No, but planned in the next 2 years	33	37/26
No, and not currently planned	46	36/62

Base: 213

Table 22: Does your authority have any Estate Agreements with registered social landlords on joint management of rented housing?

	%	Urban/rural differences %
Yes, fully integrated approach already in place	2	2/1
Yes, limited approach in place	16	20/11
No, but planned for the future	19	21/16
No, and not currently planned	63	57/72

Base: 210

Table 23: Does your authority have any plans to introduce neighbourhood management of local authority services (not just housing)?

	%	Urban/rural differences %
Yes, already in place	6	7/5
No, but planned in the next 2 years	24	32/12
No, and not currently planned	70	61/83

Base: 216

Table 24: If neighbourhood management is in place or being developed, who has the lead role within the local authority?

	%	Urban/rural differences %
Local authority housing department	48	51/38
Local authority – chief executive/corporate unit	52	49/62

Base: 64

Best Value

- 75 per cent of authorities have already undertaken reviews this year on housing services (Table 25);

- 40 per cent of planned Best Value reviews are on housing management; 12 per cent on the strategic/enabling role; 10 per cent on homelessness; 7 per cent on private sector work; and 6 per cent on housing advice (Table 26);

- 77 per cent of authorities have produced a tenant participation compact, with a further 18 per cent having this in progress (Table 27);

- 92 per cent of authorities have involved councils tenants through customer satisfaction surveys; 92 per cent through proposals for changing and improving services; 85 per cent through being involved in decisions on the housing strategy; and 81 per cent on monitoring performance (Table 28);

- 48 per cent of authorities have involved potential tenants in customer satisfaction surveys; 43 per cent on proposals for changing and improving services; 21 per cent on decisions on the housing strategy; and 16 per cent on monitoring performance (Table 29);

- 67 per cent of authorities have included working with Registered Social Landlords in their Best Value Performance Plan (Table 30)

- 79 per cent of authorities worked with RSLs on carrying out reviews of services; 70 per cent on benchmarking clubs; and 32 per cent on new approaches to tenant participation (Table 31).

Table 25: have you undertaken any Best Value reviews in relation to housing services this year?

	%	Urban/rural differences %
Yes	75	82/62
No	25	18/38

Base: 229

Table 26: Best Value reviews

This table shows analysis of all the topics mentioned by responding authorities for Best Value reviews over the next five years.

Best Value review area	%
Housing management	40
Strategic/enabling role	12
Homelessness	10
Private sector work	7
Housing advice	6
Housing needs	4
Older people	3
Sheltered housing	3
Supported housing/care & support	3
Housing benefit/welfare advice	3
Other	9

Base: 555 listed review areas from respondents

Note 1: Housing management covers mentions of housing management in general; repairs and maintenance; rents and revenue; tenant participation; allocations/lettings; housing register; tenancy management; right-to-buy; leasehold management

Note 2: **Other** includes community safety; care and repair; disability; regeneration; public health; private tenants; energy efficiency; social inclusion; housing standards.

Table 27: Has your authority produced a tenant participation compact?

	%	Urban/rural differences %
Yes, completed	77	74/83
No, but in progress	18	20/14
No, but planned in future	4	6/3

Base: 180 (excludes LSVTs)

Table 28: Have you involved council tenants in the following?

	% Yes	Urban/rural differences %
Customer satisfaction surveys	92	92/92
Proposals for changing and improving services	92	96/86
Decisions on the housing strategy	85	87/82
Arrangements in monitoring and reporting on LA performance	81	84/76

Base: 188

Table 29: Have you involved potential tenants in the following?

	% Yes	Urban/rural differences %
Customer satisfaction surveys	48	49/47
Proposals for changing and improving services	43	46/38
Decisions on the housing strategy	21	25/15
Arrangements in monitoring and reporting on LA performance	16	16/16

Base: 209

Table 30: Have you included working with Registered Social Landlords in your Best Value Performance Plan?

	%	Urban/rural differences %
Yes	67	66/67
No	33	34/33

Base: 223

Table 31: Working with RSLs on Best Value Performance Plan – what this included:

	% Yes	Urban/rural differences %
Carrying out reviews of services	79	76/86
Establishing benchmarking clubs	70	72/67
Developing new approaches to tenant participation	32	34/34

Base: 132

Choice in lettings/nominations policies

- 87 per cent of authorities have undertaken a review of allocation policies since the 1996 Housing Act (Table 32);

- 41 per cent are currently reviewing allocations policies in light of the Housing Green Paper, and a further 36 per cent plan to review this in the next 12 months (Table 33);

- 33 per cent of authorities have a Common Housing Register with RSLs, and a further 14 per cent have this planned in the next 12 months (Table 34);

- 13 per cent have a Common Allocations Policy with RSLs, and a further 11 per cent have this planned for the next 12 months (Table 35);

- 38 per cent have plans for local lettings policies, with a further 33 per cent planning to look at local lettings policies (Table 36). Of those who responded Yes, 50 per cent said they only applied to council housing, and the other 50 per cent to cross-sector housing;

- on the whole local authorities are flexible about exclusions from the housing register. 16 per cent are excluded on a permanent basis through a lack of residential qualification; 12 per cent evicted for anti-social behaviour; 5 per cent for a criminal conviction; and 3 per cent for rent arrears or other debts owed (Table 37);

- of those who are a stock transfer authority, 49 per cent have the Housing Register in-house, and 51 per cent contract it out.

Table 32: have you carried out a review of your allocation policies since the implementation of the Housing Act 1996?

	%	Urban/rural differences %
Yes	87	89/84
No	14	11/16

Base: 225

Table 33: Are you planning to review your allocations policies in the light of the Housing Green Paper?

	%	Urban/rural differences %
Yes, currently reviewing	41	46/33
Yes, planned in the next 12 months	36	30/46
No, not currently planning to review	10	12/8
Not yet decided	13	12/13

Base: 231

Table 34: Do you have a Common Housing Register with RSLs?

	%	Urban/rural differences %
Yes, in place	33	24/46
No, but planned in the next 12 months	14	15/13
No, and not currently planned	43	50/33
Not yet decided	8	11/8

Base: 231

Table 35: Do you have a Common Allocations Policy with RSLs?

	%	Urban/rural differences %
Yes, in place	13	12/14
No, but planned in the next 12 months	11	9/14
No, and not currently planned	57	57/58
Not yet decided	19	22/14

Base: 231

Table 36: Do you have, or have plans to have, any local lettings policies?

	%	Urban/rural differences %
Yes	38	43/30
Planned/ under consideration	33	32/34
No	29	25/36

Base: 225

Of those who responded 'yes', 50 per cent said they applied only to council housing, and 50 per cent said they applied to cross-sector housing.

Table 37: Do you currently exclude any of the following groups from your Housing Register?

	Permanent basis	Time limited	Until circumstances change	Not excluded
Evicted for anti-social behaviour	12	23	25	40
Evicted for rent arrears	3	16	43	38
Other debts owed	3	4	27	66
Lack of residential qualification	16	17	17	50
Criminal conviction	5	9	10	76

Base: 215

Table 38: If you are a stock transfer authority, is the Housing Register:

	%	Urban/rural differences %
In-house	49	59/43
Contracted out	51	41/57

Base: 59

Housing advice services

- 87 per cent of authorities said housing advice services were provided directly by the local authority; 50 per cent said they gave funding to advice services; 17 per cent said it was contracted out; and 10 per cent used the Community Legal Service (Table 39);

- 38 per cent of authorities are planning to expand housing advice services in light of the Housing Green Paper (Table 40).

Table 39: How are housing advice services provided within your authority?

	%	Urban/rural differences %
Provided directly by local authority	87	88/87
Contracted out	17	13/19
Using Community Legal Service	10	11/8
Funding	49	50/47

Base: 230

Table 40: Are you planning to expand housing advice services in light of Housing Green Paper?

	%	Urban/rural differences %
Yes	38	31/49
No	62	69/51

Base: 218

Appendix 1: about the survey

This survey was carried out by the LGA research team.

The questionnaires were sent to the chief executives in all 376 local authorities who provide housing services in England and Wales in November 2000 (ie not county councils). A reminder letter and additional questionnaire was sent out in January 2001. By the end of the fieldwork period in mid-February 2001, 245 local authorities had responded, representing a 65 per cent response rate.

The response rates by type of authority are shown below:

Authority type	Number of authorities	Number of returned questionnaires	% responded
Metropolitan	36	25	69
London Borough (LB)	33	21	64
Unitary authority (UA)	47	31	66
District Council (DC)	238	157	66
Welsh unitary (WU)	22	11	50
Total	**376**	**245**	**65**

The response rates by Government Office Region are shown below:

Region	Number of authorities	Number of completed questionnaires	% responded
North East (NE)	23	12	529
North West (NW)	43	32	74
Yorkshire & Humberside (Y&H)	21	11	52
East Midlands (EM)	40	25	62
West Midlands (WM)	34	20	59
South West (SW)	45	33	73
Eastern (E)	48	33	69
London (L)	33	21	64
South East (SE)	67	47	70
Wales	22	11	50
Total	**376**	**245**	**65**

The response rate by urban or rural authorities:

Region	Number of authorities	Number of completed questionnaires	% responded
Urban	230	148	64
Rural	146	97	66
Total	**376**	**245**	**65**

Based on Countryside Agency definitions of urban and rural authorities.